Ogden
O. Henry
Op. Ed.

***A MULTIVERSE OF POLITICAL HUMOR,
SOCIAL COMMENTARY AND
PLAYFUL QUIPS***

WILL TREVIER

Copyright © 2020 by Will Trevier.

All rights reserved, with the exception that any portion of this original work may be used or shared subject to and in accordance with those rights specified in the Creative Commons Attribution-NonCommercial-NoDerivatives 4.0 International Public License/CC-BY-ND 4.0. See https://creativecommons.org/licenses/by-nc-nd/4.0/legalcode.

Library of Congress Control Number: 2020941161
Library of Congress Cataloging-in-Publication Data available.

ISBN: 978-1-6629-0265-9 (Paperback)
ISBN: 978-1-6629-0266-6 (eBook)

Credits & References and Disclaimers can be found at the end of this work.

Printed in the United States of America

Published by: Sirventes Press

First published: August, 2020

10 9 8 7 6 5 4 3 2 1

The poet Ogden Nash and the short-story writer O. Henry are icons of twentieth century literature. Their famous styles of humor, revelation, amusement, and surprise are celebrated in this collection of verse. While the subject matter of this work may in part be different from the themes of these literary masters, the enduring spirit of their ingenuity and artistry lives within these pages, and their names and reputations deserve to be remembered and distinguished with a deep bow.

Ogden

O. Henry

Op. Ed.

T-Rump thinks himself a T-Rex,
A resemblance old Dino rejects,
Except for their methane
The size of their pea brain
And their primitive, small-hand defects.

Michele Obama's
The cat's pajamas
Modeling charm, inspiration and love
Iron equipoise in a red velvet glove.

Most vegans now think it's a sign
That alt-protein is found to be fine.
Hence new promos "Got Soy?"
Earn hoi fives from polloi
And cattle who won't walk the line.

Denies that his mouth's running wild
Denies that his Party is riled
Denies global warming
Denies he's been Stormying
Denies he's Adolf's secret child.

In sickness and health we do take
New meaning from those we forsake.
To put out our "I"s
Makes Us the main prize,
Igniting our "selfs" at the stake.

The moment's masseur of disguise
Passes truth off as so many lies.
One hopes that the law
Will take a buzz saw
To the fraud that's become his franchise.

∞

Ouroboros eats self without trace,
A compulsive, insane *coup de grace*.
Hence infinity's fated
To be terminated,
Devoured in a deadly arms race.

forward to the past
our elected frankenstein
my god, "It's Alive"!!

GOP's where rank greed gets congrats.
Johnny Rebs of the rich in cocked hats.
Ma and Pa you enslave
As Abe turns in his grave.
A racket of mean 'ristocrats.

We strut down the street in Versace
Coyly flirting with men playing bocce.
We toss our coiffed curls
And flash them our pearls,
Then laugh at our next *kaffee klatsche*.

Maladjusted, this poor little Trump
Flaps his gums to conceal a wee stump.
He lies about taxes
And alternative "factes,"
While the nation's great past is his chump.

Donald Trump ain't a Churchill, that's clear.
No silk verse from that vulgar swine's ear.
So with fascist effront'ry
He gives nothing to country
But mud(slinging), debt, roil, and fear.

A crass mammal who's slung campaign muck
Named himself a white swan (cobs' bad luck).
But a keen Uncle Sam
Saw a trumpeter sham
That was naught but a Muscovite duck.

True sermons aren't science but art
Oft preaching puts hearse before cart.
Brimstone your pieties
Bonfire anxieties,
Speak not from the head, but the heart.

anti-immigrants
henchmen of hypocrisy
like white on reichs

Goll-darn dyslexia, fie!
Staying on task wits our try.
So bass ackwards are we
That life's order needs be
Blessed by the Lama Dalai.

Depravity, terror, disease,
Napalm, cartels, WMDs,
Nuclear blasts,
Gun deaths en masse,
Hell, Dante's been brought to his knees.

Forget abs, forget glutes, forget pecs
Or an invite upstairs to read Brecht.
Hormones are the pastors
Of Johnson and Masters,
For pheromones catalyze sex.

A bomb plugs a plotter's vote holes
Untrumpled by broken rice bowls
Geigered whirlwinds of weep
"Holocost" on the cheap
A contemptible seller of seouls.

Trump's conduct is ever ironic
Deserving responses sardonic.
He's none but riffraff
Always good for a laugh.
Quite droll, were he not so demonic.

Mistletoe's hung 'round the year
O'er the desk of the Chief-in-Cashier.
Since his chairs are for rent,
'Tis an emolument
To sit while you're kissing his rear.

virtue's predator
a nation raped by his greed
donald j. gekko

pirouettes imper'll'd
plies of passing primas
ballet's limbphomas

The most recent big app like <u>so</u> fails,
We're informed by our newborns' emails.
No more sucking of thumbs
That block texting to chums.
The next market, *in utero* sales.

No matter if Sunni or Shiite
Most Moslems are fiends of the far right.
Hijab or Keffiyeh,
You're not welcome he-ah
Say racists whose bilge is their birthright.

Sleep comes so seldom O Lord
In a household where dirt is deplored,
'Cause my nightmares abound
That on waking I'm found
To be washed, dried, folded, and drawer'd.

A Hick's Double Acrostic

Tantrump's persona
Reason's treason
Ungoverned melodrama
Maladroit distemper
Pernicious pettiness
Shameless imbecile

Though sent draft deferrals somehow
The reason Trump's service went south
To be frank his deceit
Was not really his feet
'Twas the 4-F disease foot in mouth.

Gigabyte, terabyte, yottabyte,
Growth of mem'ry is way out of sight.
Programs used to be yar.
Now it's just that they are
Not a bit, not a byte, but a blight.

Neato missiles fly fast in the air.
Super Duper! Gee Whiz! I declare.
Gotta pony as well
And my ray-gun is swell.
The Joint Chiefs are in total despair.

Mein Hair-do whose head's out to lunch
Ein Bratwurst who's bullied the bunch
Now acquited of crimes
Without reasons or rhymes.
Truth purged *mit* a quick sucker punch.

Double, double, trump and trouble
Pustules grow whilst 'postles grovel.
Fake Macbeth from witches' broth
Struts the stage, till shuffled off.

Tomorrows and tomorrows wait
As bloodied hands doth meet their fate
Whence voters guised as Birnam pyre
Deceived, betrayed, shouldst say "You're fired."

A senile accountant's worst sign
A Jack Benny abuse of straight-line.
In its terminal stage
One depletes one's own age,
So life's book value stays thirty-nine.

alt-rightist anthrax
combustive conservatives
short-fused white pow(d)er

Trump claims it's a laugh when he's lied
Then jumps in a Foxhole to hide.
So there's not much suspense,
His big legal defense
Will be "I'm just a joke," when he's tried.

procuring the sublime
meets with punishment often
more than fits the crime

Dystopia

Genocide's just no way to behave.
There's no profit in such a crime wave.
If you lash them as slaves,
You'll save bullets and graves.
A land of the free and a home of the brave.

Use of "meta" should be much more sparse
By hauteurs whose patois is a farce.
Their lexical vanity
Will test tact and sanity
Till the rest of us say "kiss my parse."

siroccos of hate
chevys rust, baseballs shatter
mom's apple pie sours

Op. Ed. is a paean to speech,
Whether essay, or assay, or preach,
Tirade or crusade,
Or spoofed pasquinade,
An evocative printed pastiche.

Reason and truth are now scoffed
By those whose big mouths runneth off.
Justice is might
And history's shite.
The new man of the hour, a dumbkopf.

With new tax breaks for those in the pink
Social safeguards are pushed past the brink.
This state-sponsored lootin'
Apes a Prez just like Putin
Marking Trump as the true Missing Link.

Self-Own Syntax

A waltz in three feet, marking dactylic time.
A one and a two, in a pert paradigm.
Then prance dimetered lines
'Fore a last twirl of trines
Where a limerick ends with a laugh and a rhyme.

battered supporters
suff'ring "tariffic" abuse
slink back to daddy

What evils lurk in smirks that loom
In ghouls' sly foxy death-row grins?
It's satan's sure-fire cures that doom
A fool's hydroxychlorquines.

The law,
safer from flaw,
when freed from convention
and political dimension
tension.

Compared to a CinC who's a liar
And a Colonel Klink source of satire,
A Top Brass named Barak,
Forged from much sterner stock,
Commanded with grace under fire.

Our First Swine who's a cheat and a liar
A Poor-Me prototype of town crier
Is clearly projected
To be re-elected
When pigs all become frequent fliers.

*Caution: What follows depicts a depth of
shock, anger, loss, anxiety, and horror,
raw and unrelieved.*

schoolhouse homicides
skull splatters of innocence
god's concealed permit

When the word comes on down from the Docs
And life breaks onto shoals and sharp rocks,
Pry yourself from your fear,
Tell the fates to stand clear,
Or you'll drop a big house on their pox.

white house spin cycles
a new tide of old soaps
the days of our lies

A scratch-obsessed son of an itch
Rants the State's on a hunt for a witch.
The nation's First Cad
Ever sniv'ling "So sad."
A whiner with imperfect pitch.

Sciatica makes my life swell
With nerve pain like I was in hell.
If opiods crater,
Then sooner or later
I'll be put in a small padded cell.

Common decency has suffered a hijack
At the hands of a White House led rat pack.
A paranoid schiz
And other misfits
Have driven our nation to Prozac.

technology, new
opiate of the masses
america's got latent

A state or condition stems from
The suffix we all know as "dom."
So if "freedom's" being free,
Then T's "rumpdom" would be
The condition of being a bum.

From a rib, it is preached one begets
A soulmate to sing life's duets.
If this bliss from above
Is the source of true love,
Then shrines should be built to our pets.

Of those with the President's ear
So many have heard his Bronx cheer.
Whether you've quit
Or put up with the Nit,
It's a twilight of loathing and fear.

Quand nos spirits, clear *têtes*, and warm hearts
Sync with instinct, then Monsieur Descartes'
Je pense, thus I am
Fait un flawed *épigramme*
Sans life's *harmonie* sung in four *partes*.

u.s. gestapo
bordering on *kristallnachts*
amerikan *schICEss.*

Donald Dick, head of state, so despised,
A limp prick that is plum undersized.
Dubbed as two pounds of brag
In a one pound scumbag.
A fat slimeball that's offal disguised.

One Donald J. Scrooge
The country's First Stooge.
What goes around as ghastly trolls
Comes back as ghosts of future polls.

If "Indifference" is said to be "Meh"
And "Disgust" only comes out as "Bleh,"
A creative wordsmith
Could upgrade urban myth
So "Not giving a sh*t" would be "Sheh."

Paradise

Conflagration's no problem, he spake,
Fixing blame is the best fire break.
Dislocation and loss,
Just combustible dross.
In the meantime, make do with a rake.

white house drama queen
ersatz exhibitionist
primadon peacock

Langsam und schmachtend, perforce,
An orchestral notation of sorts.
"Slow and yet yearning"
For musicians discerning.
To the rest of us just coded Morse.

One Word Wanker

As a name-calling turd he's typecast, see,
A hypocrite who acts all aghast, he
Howls that he's hurt
By other folk's dirt
When his own tongue is stuck up his nasty.

I'm frightened for my inner soul
I'm at a crossroads cleft
So shaken by my inner soul
I'm at a crossroads cleft
A dreaded anger's on the right
And deep despair is on the left.

Abuse has cracked a heartless whip
Despair by other name
Abuse has cracked its curséd whip
Despair by other name
True, I've survived for many years
The hidden cost, a burning shame.

Oh, bitter pain comes out at dusk
While fear creeps up at night
Oh, grievous wounds crawl out at dusk
Then fear creeps up at night
For stigma throws an uppercut
And shattered hopes put out your lights.

New York madman confirms urban lore
Shooting farmers to advance a trade war.
Despite the disaster,
They tell their Red master,
Please sir, may we have some more.

Gratitude has its allure.
How sweet to embrace a savior.
But as grounds for a match,
It's a sure booby hatch
Absent mystery that's love's *force majeure*.

Sartre's impostor

Of his sins, Pride's considered essential
By our profligate ponce presidential.
In his twisted mind's steeple
He swears "Hell's other people."
Conceited, profane, existential.

Dodging capitol crimes, the Deceiver
Who's sickened us all with swamp fever
Might grant our fond hope
As described by the trope
Of a hangman who pulls his own leaver.

fired glazes cool
colored reincarnations
porcelain kismet

A taxman, a King, George the Third,
Dismissed our tax pleas as absurd.
Now our Party of Teas
Displays George's porph'ries
And like him will soon be interred.

Think the Rubicon can be re-crossed?
Seek profit when par'dise is lost?
Then the codes of Confucius
And the Greek guides of hubris
Will doom <u>you</u> to be hung, not the cost.

private equity
planet earth's products and jobs
glycophosphated

Immigration, a viral disease,
Shithole shudders, and pussy payees,
A convulsion of lies,
A demented disguise,
Democracy sweating DTs.

It's such that you just can't be serious.
You're mad, lost your mind, so delirious.
If the writing of verse
Is a herpes-like curse,
Try some iamb acyclovirious.

Stephen Colbert
Trump's *mal de mer*
Ridicule, mockery, lampoon, and barb
Ingenious mind in a court jester's garb.

If religion gives meaning to life
Through compassion and soothing of strife,
Then no matter the Being,
Supreme or All-Seeing,
She'd rather you worship your wife.

Le gros Chef daily serving manure
A crude kook who's a Mc™Epicure.
His whole foods are Swiss cheese,
So quick, bring the check please.
We're tired of this rank *stupe du jour*.

You've elected a booster
And got a surprise,
A bankrupted carny
And barker of lies.

Many rugs cov'ring hair that is left
Are like fuzz waiting sentence for theft.
If you seek a reprieve,
Try a different hair weave
From a loom with a 4-heddle weft.

Trumped-up Truisms:

Nothing spoils a lie like limpidity.

Propriety is politics perverted.

'rump gives 'rse a bad rep.

the fake 45
elevates unto statesman
gaffeboy 43

The sun's near high noon
And all down the block
Not a creature was stirring
Except the darn clock.
We seem to be drugged,
A square key to round lock,
But we're really recov'ring
From DST shock.

If morphology's dull and conventional
And you search for a shape more inventional,
Then try to define
A form without line
For a thrill not two/three dimensional.

You'd think it not hard to deduce
The green color of spewed gastric juice
Would sound like it's puce.
But just *entre nous*,
It more closely resembles chartreuse.

Some say love is a ruse, a red-herring
A condition of which they're despairing.
But those who'd throw hisses
Aren't kin to your kisses
To which there is just no comparing.

When foiled, a thief's new defense
Tout Latin and twist common sense.
Ain't nuttin' got taken
As part of duh break-in,
So, no *quid pro quo*, no offense.

A profaner of public Who's Whos
Having gargled with *Eau* of the Loos,
His faults remain hidden
By insults unbidden.
The schlump's an *ad hominem* muse.

A farce, infantile and perverse.
Ill-humor that needs a wet nurse.
Trump's twitter eruptions
Are tiffs of connuptions.
Blow comedy couldn't get worse.

california
heterodox habitat
yea, there be dragons

Facebook's covert fatal flaw
To rule social networks as Shah,
Exposing our names
For unscrupulous aims,
Inciting its own Anti-Fa.

A few who engender new trends
Seek attachment as more than just friends.
A sacrament starts
'Tween those with same parts
And ends with a life love transcends.

grandiosity
delusional phallusy
big twat, no chattel

Endless robo calls claim as their motto
We'll make you a cash-strapped castrato.
These mechanized dialers
Are sham-faced beguilers
Perpetrating the crime: Grand Theft Auto.

a loony potus
official orifice holder
our nation's loophole

London's Circus saw rot as spy poise
Spawning Philby's five Kremlin decoys.
Front-line agents were shot,
But the true guilty lot
Were rear networks of rancid old boys.

As some hot-blooded, Homeric creatures
Are subdued by a goddess's features,
So my Minotaur heart, love,
You've vanquished like one of
Those *veni* and *vidi* and *vici*-ers.

We're numbed by his customs insanal
And habitual acts inhumanal.
But normalized sin
Harks back to Berlin
And evil's embrace of the banal.

Entrenched behind fence do they hunker
While The Donald's campaign comes-a-clunker
As Trump's D-Day draws near
His tense staff's biggest fear
Is their <u>own</u> blood being shed in the Bunker.

I hear the sound of sacred chords
A trill of life replacing words.

Cough in one's face and no tellin'
How quickly you'll have your own cell in
Death row's separate section
For lethal injection
Befitting a pandemic felon.

The A.G.'s appointed Barrista
Whose briefs smell of legal *turista*
Displays no moral sense
Donald Trump's his conscience
A sinister type of *fascista*.

Panic strikes when thinking life ceases
In a hole that consumes all its pieces.
Synchronicity proves, though,
There's more past the late show,
So extinction's a poor exegesis.

collateral death
remorseless rules of combat
real life blame of drones

If your homonym knowledge goes AWOL
Brush up, don't just throw in the towel.
Diuresis/Dieresis
Their sameness is specious.
Beware you don't pee on a vowel.

Trump's past vices create apprehensia
That his sickness keeps gaining momentia
'Long with cognitive crumblings
And neur'logical stumblings
Diagnosis: Syph'litic Dementia.

Post hoc ergo propter hoc
Logic's chronic stumbling block
Since day follows night, you'd think it implies
That dark causes light – a faulty surmise.

Donald Trump, today's groom of apartheid
Espousing the evils of white pride,
Weds in bloody betrothing
Of new fear and old loathing
John Birch as a born-again war bride.

Talking head organ grinders excite
The monkey to mug the spotlight.
As the chimp shows his arse,
We're benumbed by the farce
Though it's slapstick we help underwrite.

we few. we happy
few. we big band of brothers.
bill shakespeare's swing set

Recent protesters' daylight nightmare
Saw God trumped in a brutal fanfare
Lafayette Park
A nation's landmark
Reborn as Tiananmen Square.

Guli

A shady sayer of sooth
Strives to sucker the smug and uncouth
Through an ethical con
As a fake paragon
And shyster of relative truth.

Sean Patrick Hannity
Slag of insanity
Trump's caddie of clap, brown-nosed and blistery
Purveyor of pap, hann-jobbing history.

English usage is in such a mess
The word "less" is confused, I confess,
With "fewer" so much.
We best craft a crutch
By creating the term "fewerless."

Trump, Donald John
Meglomoron
Gifting barbed-wire camps to all those without cash
From a goose-stepping tyrant devoid of mustache.

A font by the name Comic Sans
Whose past fame once outpaced also-rans
Lately can't get a gig
'Cause it's so infra dig.
Oh well, *sic transit gloria*, fans.

In adjudging a foul falsifier
Who's a devious, whole truth denier,
On the political spectrum
Of the voting electrum
Everyone's left of a liar.

White Hosing truth is a joy
For a spoiled, petty, rich, little boy
Who rips off its wings
And molests its pure things.
When it dies, why it's only a toy.

Dialectical Dismissal

Doing what's right can get gory
A path to White House purgatory.
First you get snarks
From the Trumper of Marx,
Then off'd, as not slave to hi(s)tory.

For many it's just the law straw,
A profession that sticks in their craw.
So your standing won't lapse
Better keep under wraps
That you're licensed to practice the law.

Democracy's been undermined.
Voting rights are no longer enshrined.
Cast a ballot. Don't wait.
In Chicago, cast eight.
Save yourself, your kids, humankind.

whitewash of white house
red senators putin-proud
our politburo

Sometimes death's a love's severance
Giving birth to life's reverence.

Gun-toting marchers' dark tasks
Simply bottle bad wine in new casks.
Bankrolled, to be blunt,
Like an old Commie Front
By backers in Astroturf masks.

To those whose crazed calls cause cold sweats
Or who email with snide epithets,
You're a coward and wimp,
A pestilent pimp,
If your address ain't part of your threats.

a wake of frost

tears in the writer
grieving tears in the reader
obituary

Its players are legion and fabled,
A Gentleman's Game it is labeled.
But "You Da Man" shouts
From disorderly mouts
Seem distractions that Golf has enabled.

"Pin the Tail," an old game at a party
Has evolved to be more arty-smarty.
Now we play "Pick the Lump,"
A mute Pence or dense Trump.
Our nation's new Laurel and Hardy.

Hedonists bare no surprises
Humping away in high-rises.
One such a slob
With big head and small nob
Diddles while Rome polarizes.

acumen/anger
empathy/egotism
opposites detract

Prisons are racial enclaves,
'Nother name for plantations of slaves.
Money's the key
For some set scot-free.
For the rest, it's a black home of graves.

hispanic cleansing
in ICE storms brown lives shatter
donald's dragnet days

New lingo has tarnished the crown
Of sound thought and sage acts of renown.
Now self-serving themes
And throw-the-dice schemes
Are enthroned by the dare "doubling-down."

Decency's lost on the lout.
ROI is the crack in his clout.
So, to cause him distress
Rile his renters and guests
With the back-at-ya chant "Lock 'Em Out."

Soccer all-stars have nothing on thee,
A black day due to joint surgery.
Beckham's foot on the left
Is now bleak and bereft.
It can't match a bionic, left knee.

brexitannia
imperial nostalgia
old empire zombies

Schiller's Angst

Combating stupidity's curse
The gods are in vain and averse,
For their power is lost
Till we all pay the cost
When the body count turns for the worse.

Animal Husbandry

Debauchery's trademarked Trump's name.
Fornication appears his great aim.
Though he seeks re-election,
Better yet, vivisection
To "fix" the lounge lizard's sick fame.

Comrade Trump's robbed our country half-blind
Leaving most in a broke state of mind.
While his fat riches grow,
We've got nothing to show
But his *botinok* up our behind.

generosity
hidden socialbond value
higher shareprice

Donald's Debility

Vocab senility
Racial hostility
Macho fragility
Russian servility
Low-count motility

Oh please Doc, inject thiopental
To deal with my pain plainly dental.
Though my teeth need relief,
Oral surg'ry's pure grief.
This maxillo-mess makes me mental.

To good Suth'ners your lies are chagrined
Fetid falsehoods that witness you've sinned.
To be perfectly clear
Donald, frankly my dear,
Let your bullshit be gone with the wind.

The Donald and the Dunderhead

"My time has come," The Donald pled,
Denying many things,
Like lies, allies, and tax replies,
And secret sexist flings,
Or that a man's morality
He measures in ca-chings.

The Donald said: "I'm loved by all,
A favored Lord of Flies.
It's no contest, they all profess,
It's me they idolize.
So it's not odd when they quote God,
I've got to roll my eyes."

"The Dunderhead has got no sense,
'The Pence' by other name.
His wits are flushed. His mind is mush.
The lame that's brought him fame.
A low IQ. He's got no clue.
He puts insane to shame."

"I'm your fist," The Donald vowed.
"Your hates I hold so tight.
The foreign trash, whose kids we cache,
My wall will keep from sight."
He then let fly: "It's do or fry.
Our motto's 'Might makes fright.'"

"Huge tax relief," The Donald pledged
At corporate boards' behest.
"Poor billionaires, their market shares,
Alas, they're so depressed.
The public even gets a buck
To make them feel they're blessed."

"At times The Pence will try to preach
As though he's heard my Call.
To slap him some is so much fun.
He's rather farcical.
His speech is even weirder for
He has no mouth at all."

(continued on next page)

"I'm not that guy," The Donald lied.
"My conscience has not care.
Despite the claims, I've brought no shame
Upon the sex so fair.
If you don't like, go take a hike.
It's strictly my affair."

"I've run through staff," The Donald laughed.
"There's no one left to see.
I'd rather not be on the spot
And hire family.
But place your bets that my last Ex
Will be the next AG."

"A shell game on 5th Avenue
Is but my true success.
Forgive my sad misspellingses.
Forget the Mueller mess.
Let's dine at eight, 10 Gs a plate,
But say my name for less."

"Those dirty Docs should catch smallpox,
I hope they hear me screech.
No mask or distance helps existence,
Nor quarantine I breach.
'Cause COVID deaths won't stop unless
You people guzzle bleach."

"The shutdown, tariffs, ICE-led raids,
So many lives I've wrecked.
It brings me so much comfort when
The government's unchecked.
I smile to know my fortunes flow
From one religious sect."

The Donald and the Dunderhead,
They weep into their beers.
To see collapse and its impacts,
Bemoaning their careers.
And this is passing strange because
They haven't any tears.

Once a frantical frenzy of fish
Took a bath with much splash and more splish.
Such sweet bedtime stories
Soothe young daughters' worries.
Sleepy smiles are your favorite wish.

Peeved that some poems seem too drastic
As though you've been deemed pederastic?
If you dream they're a sleight
Or a scheme of false light,
Don't get steamed, 'cause I'm just being "sarcastic."

Humpty D. Trumpty's the gall
To claim he's not in for a fall.
But like Rich Number Three,
His last words will be:
My realm, Oh my realm, for a wall.

NOTES

Among the thoughts readers may have are questions whether poems in this book contain errors in spelling and usage. Please know that for purposes of humor and poetic license, the spellings in each poem are intended. For example, words such as "Hosing," "leaver," "connuptions," "mouts" and the mischievious "misspellingses" have all been conscious choices. At times, some words are actually enclosed in quotation marks if the spelling is especially unusual. Normal pronunciation has also at times been whimsically adapted to a poem's rhyme scheme. For instance, in one poem the word "grace" (in the phrase "coup de grace"), which in deference to its French origin is usually pronounced more like "graz," has been playfully used to rhyme with the words "trace" and "arms race."

Also important are some observations about the book's poetic forms; the most predominant of which are limericks and haiku. The choice of these two forms was primarily based on a common characteristic: brevity. The demand for brevity in our current patterns of communication seems to be an inextricable part of our lives. Whether by way of social media texting, headline news, sound bytes, and even emoticons, abbreviation has become a hallmark in the conveyance of meaning. The brevity of limericks and haiku allows this work not just to be memorable and easily understood, but, in today's world, more widely accepted and enjoyed in comparison to their longer, poetic cousins. In addition, both forms have been tailored so that in most cases the last line contains an unexpected idea, revealing thought, or humorous twist. This strategy was incorporated not only as a method of modeling the work of the two authors to whom the book is dedicated, but also of giving the audience an incentive to continue reading, rewarding them for doing so with the pleasure of a surprise.

While both poetic forms have this important similarity, readers will note that both have also been markedly adapted. Just like beginning a story with the words "Once upon a time...", the well-known rhythm of a limerick allows readers to relax and prepare to be entertained. But what comes next is an alteration of the form, conveying a different kind of message of somewhat greater literary note and with the potential of engaging further thought. This adapted form might be called a "literick," in which for symbolic purposes culture plays the clown by engrafting more literate themes onto a rather burlesque poetic form. But, no matter its name, the original profile of this verse has been elevated hopefully to appeal to a wider audience and offer another type of surprise for its readers.

The traditional focus of haiku has also been transformed. Substituted for its customary accentuation of nature, aesthetics, and image, the haiku in this work have instead spotlighted ideas. No disrespect is meant to the honored elegance and classical construction of this form. But in this volume the more esoteric peaks in the style of this poetry have been partially leveled, perhaps garnering greater appreciation of the meaning within its lines and allowing the brevity of the form to be accepted by a larger readership.

The manner in which these poems are presented also deserves a small comment. Throughout this book, poems embodying political and social commentary are commingled with poems reflecting themes of daily life. While poems in these two categories could have been grouped into different sections of the book, doing so would have risked impairing the element of surprise, by cueing the audience to what type of poem came next, potentially causing a writer's nightmare – a reader's fatigue. Shuffling the poems limited this possibility.

Just as importantly, there is a larger motive at work. It is well accepted that for some time our country has been experiencing an intensified level of incivility, for which the reasons are immense. In fact, many poems in this book concern the ongoing frustration that underlies the challenge of civil discourse. For example, this work is one of a countless number of books revealing the harms that so many people, organizations, businesses, institutions, and global neighbors have suffered at the hands of the Trump administration. Accordingly, by interweaving poems of a political/social character with those reflecting aspects of normal life, a small hope is offered to ease the effects of this onslaught of dissension. This is not to be dismissive in any way of the need to be vigilant, but is rather intended to give voice to a recognition that our normal routines are also important and worthy of acknowledgment, despite the continual abuse they're absorbing. Perhaps it's a way of reducing the social distance among different people, and between disparate parts of ourselves. However, as noted, it's truly but a small hope.

CREDITS & REFERENCES

Ogden Nash and O. Henry (William Sydney Porter) are treasured American humorists, whose writing styles serve as a foundation of this work.

Hannah Arendt, a 20th century German-American writer and political theorist is credited for having coined the phrase the "banality of evil" associated with her 1963 book <u>Eichmann in Jerusalem: A Report on the Banality of Evil</u>. This phrase has been transformed in this work.

"Astrotufing" is a political term that refers to concealing the sponsor of an orchestrated campaign to create the false impression it has public support. This term is referenced in this work.

John L. Balderston, Francis Edward Faragoh, and Garrett Fort are credited for writing the 1931 horror film Frankenstein, directed by James Whale, from which comes the famous line "It's Alive" that is referenced in this work. Credit is also due Mary Shelley who wrote the widely read 1818 novel <u>Frankenstein</u> on which the film is generally based.

David Beckham is considered one of the great English football players of his generation. He is referenced in this work.

Jack Benny, the 20th century comedian and entertainer is credited for his long-running gag perpetually celebrating his 39th birthday to avoid getting older. This comedy routine is referenced in this work.

The John Birch Society has been described as a radical right, arch-conservative group, considered a fringe element in the 1960s/1970s, that at the time espoused certain conspiracy theories which again may be influencing the conservative party. This organization has been referenced in this work.

Julius Caesar, the 1st century (BCE) Roman emperor is credited for the quotation "Veni, Vidi, Vici," translated as "I came, I saw, I conquered." This phrase is referenced and transformed in this work.

Winston Churchill, the extraordinary 20th century British Prime Minister who served in this capacity during and after World War II, is credited for the famous quotation from his May 13, 1940 speech to the House of Commons: "I have nothing to offer but blood, toil, tears and sweat." This quotation has been transformed in this work.

Rene Descartes, the 18th century French mathematician and philosopher, is credited for the quotation: "Je pense, donc je suis" (also in Latin

307

as: "Cogito, ergo sum"), which has usually been translated as: "I think, therefore I am." This quotation has been transformed in this work.

Charles Dickens, the 19th century English writer, is credited for the widely known quotation "Please sire, I want some more," from his book Oliver Twist. A form of this quotation is referenced and transformed in this work.

Charles Dodgson, better known as Lewis Carroll, the 19th century English writer, is credited for the poem: "The Walrus and The Carpenter." This poem has been transformed in this work.

Robert Frost, the famous 20th century American poet, is credited for the quotation: "No tears in the writer, no tears in the reader. No surprise in the writer, no surprise in the reader." A portion of this quotation has been transformed in this work.

"Force majeure" is a French phrase, frequently used in contract law, loosely translated as "unforeseeable circumstances," and often associated with the idea of an Act of God, that is unpredictable, external and irresistible. This phrase is referenced in this work.

Got Milk?™ is a noted American advertising slogan and registered trademark licensed by the California Milk Processing Board to whom credit is given for this slogan, which is transformed in this work.

Laurel and Hardy were an early 20th century iconic comedy act known for slapstick routines popularized in Hollywood films. They are referenced in this work.

John Lithgow, the popular, current American actor and writer, is credited for publicizing the connection between Humpty Dumpty and Donald Trump in his book Dumpty, copyrighted in November, 2019. A poem included in Ogden, O. Henry Op. Ed., which poem was written prior to the publication of Mr. Lithgow's book, makes a somewhat similar association, though it primarily refers to a famous quotation in the Shakespearean play Richard III. Though neither the book Dumpty, nor any portion of its poems, are included or transformed in this work, unfailing credit needs be given to Mr. Lithgow for promoting this humorous connection.

John Le Carré, the pen name of 20th-21st century British espionage novelist David John Moore Cromwell, is credited for the fictional name of the headquarters of British secret service, known in many of his novels as the "Circus." This term is referenced in this work.

William H. Masters and Virginia E. Johnson were a team of 20th century American researchers who published studies helping to understand human sexual response. They are referenced in this work.

McDonald's[™] is a registered trademark, as is its related letters Mc[™] in relation to food and other items in the United States. McDonald's[™] is credited for its related letters Mc[™], which are referenced and transformed in this work.

Clement Clarke Moore, a 19th century American writer, is credited for the poem widely known as "Twas the Night Before Christmas," which has been transformed in this work.

John Paul Sartre, the 20th century French writer and a major proponent of the philosophy of existentialism, is credited for the quotation: "Hell is other people," which is referenced in this work.

Friedrich Schiller, the 18th century German writer and philosopher, is credited for the quotation, generally translated as: "Against stupidity, the gods themselves contend in vain." A form of this quotation is referenced in this work.

William Shakespeare, the renowned 16th century poet and playwright, is credited for the plays <u>Macbeth</u>, <u>Richard III</u>, and <u>Henry V</u>. Well-known phrases, quotations, and references from these plays, have been used and in some cases transformed in this work.

The Latin phrase "Sic transit gloria mundi," translated as "So goes the glory of the world," and suggesting the concept of fading grandeur, is referenced and transformed in this work.

Versace is the trade name of a leading Italian fashion design company creating and distributing a variety of luxury and other products worldwide.

Stanley Weiser, Oliver Stone, and/or Oaxatal Productions, Inc., or its/their successors, are credited for the iconic 1983 American movie <u>Wall Street</u> and one of its main characters Gordon Gekko, whose name is transformed in this work.

References to other persons and terms referenced in this work are not included here, given that they may be considered sufficiently well-known and understood.

DISCLAIMERS

This work in part contains poems relating to public officials and public figures, named or suggested. Some of the poems are celebratory, others not. The content of all such poems is based on opinion, humor or exaggeration, and is to be read in the context of statements by and about, and the history, character, activities or beliefs of, such persons in their capacity as public officials or public figures. Where pertinent, the content of these poems also represents political speech made in connection with matters of public concern or in furtherance of an exercise of constitutional rights to free speech in connection with issues of public concern or about the performance of public life or duties by such public officials and public figures. The tenor and context of all poems in this work relating to public officials and public figures is also intended to negate any impression that anything herein is asserted as an objective fact, that the figurative and exaggerated language of this work further negates any such impression, and that all statements, opinions and implications from these statements and opinions, expressed about such public officials and public figures are not intended to state actual facts, do not state actual facts, and/or are not susceptible of being proven true or false.

Fair Use Notice. This work may contain copyrighted material, the use of which has in some cases not been specifically authorized by the copyright owners. Material in this work is in part included as commentary on social and political issues, which in cases where it has not been specifically authorized, it is believed constitutes a fair use of such copyrighted material as provided for in Section 107 of the US Copyright law. In those few cases in which this work may employ such copyrighted material, the work provides transformative elements that add something new with a different purpose or character to, and not substituting for, the original use of the copyrighted material. Further, only a very small portion has been excerpted from any such copyrighted material. It is believed that in this work the transformative nature and limited amount of any copyrighted material that may be used without specific authorization will also not negatively affect the market value of such material.

If you wish to use copyrighted material from this work for purposes of your own that go beyond "fair use," you must obtain permission from the copyright owner.

ABOUT THE AUTHOR

WILL TREVIER has experienced a variety of occupational cultures, received a number of degrees, and been a tireless student of his wife's teaching and intuition. Enlivened by words, he is an enduring admirer of humor and irony and for many years has enjoyed writing for personal pleasure and professional purpose. He collects various art forms and seems forever to be building shelves to house an expanding book collection. He has lived in Washington, D.C., the Midwest, and the Pacific Northwest, and he and his wife have shared their homes with a succession of four-legged friends who have enriched the family with generosity and love over many lifetimes.

However, presenting any description of accomplishments and activities based solely on one's own efforts would be impertinent, for the life described above cannot be separated from the influence of many others. This includes new friends made in the completion of this work, old friends and life-long friends who are joined at the heart, those who've helped resurrect a new life, loved ones passed whose spirits are still present, and one whose wisdom and grace will forever be celebrated within these pages. The lives of all are encircled in this biography.